ONE QUESTION A DAY FOR KIDS

365 Q&A A DAY JOURNAL FOR KIDS

THIS JOURNAL BELONGS TO:

DAY 1

WOULD YOU RATHER LIVE TO BE 100, OR BE A BILLIONAIRE AND ONLY LIVE 50 YEARS?

DAY 2

WOULD YOU RATHER HAVE TO EAT KETCHUP ON EVERYTHING, OR KETCHUP ON NOTHING EVER AGAIN?

DAY 3

WOULD YOU RATHER SEE THE GREAT PYRAMIDS OR THE GREAT WALL OF CHINA?

DAY 4

WHAT IS YOUR FAVORITE SEASON OF THE YEAR?

DAY 5

WHY DO YOU LIKE YOUR FAVORITE FOOD? WHAT MAKES IT SPECIAL?

DAY 6

IF YOU WENT ON A JUNGLE SAFARI, WHAT WOULD YOU BE MOST EXCITED TO SEE OR DO?

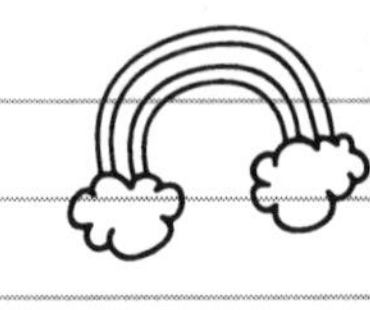

DAY 7

WHAT IS YOUR FAVORITE GAME TO PLAY?

DAY 8

IF YOU FOUND A $20 BILL, WOULD YOU TRY TO FIND ITS OWNER OR KEEP IT?

DAY 9

WHAT WOULD YOU DO IF YOU GOT TO SWITCH PLACES WITH YOUR PARENTS FOR A DAY?

DAY 10

ARE YOU GOOD AT KEEPING SECRETS?

DAY 11

WHAT DOES IT MEAN TO BE A GOOD FRIEND TO SOMEONE?

DAY 12

DO YOU WORK BETTER ALONE OR ON A TEAM?

DAY 13

IF YOU BUILT A NEW CITY, WHAT WOULD IT LOOK LIKE?

DAY 14

WOULD YOU BE MORE EXCITED TO GET TO SCUBA DIVE TO THE BOTTOM OF THE OCEAN, OR PARACHUTE OUT OF AN AIRPLANE?

DAY 15

WHAT IS THE FIRST THING YOU THINK OF WHEN YOU HEAR THE WORD "WARM"?

DAY 16

WHAT IS YOUR LEAST FAVORITE VEGETABLE?

DAY 17

IF YOU HAD TO GIVE UP ONE THING FROM YOUR ROOM, WHAT WOULD YOU CHOOSE?

DAY 18

DO YOU HAVE ANY SPECIAL TALENTS?

WHAT IS THE PRETTIEST PLACE ON EARTH?

DAY 20

IF YOU LIVED ON A FARM, WHAT WOULD YOU WANT TO GROW?

DAY 21

WHAT MAKES YOU FEEL SAFE?

DAY 22

IF YOU COULD SEE INTO THE FUTURE FOR ONLY ONE DAY, WHAT DAY WOULD YOU WANT TO SEE?

DAY 23

DO YOU LIKE THANKSGIVING OR VALENTINE'S DAY BETTER?

DAY 24

DO YOU THINK KIDS SHOULD BE REQUIRED TO GO TO SCHOOL? WHY OR WHY NOT?

DAY 25

WHAT IS YOUR FAVORITE KIND OF MUSIC?

DAY 26

WHAT IS YOUR FAVORITE THING TO DRAW?

HAVE YOU EVER STAYED AT A HOTEL? WHAT WAS IT LIKE?

DAY 28

WHAT IS YOUR FAVORITE MYTHICAL CREATURE?

DAY 29

IF YOU COULD BREAK ANY WORLD RECORD, WHICH ONE WOULD IT BE?

DAY 30

INVENT A NEW HOLIDAY AND DESCRIBE IT

DAY 31

DO YOU THINK FLYING CARS WILL BE A THING SOMEDAY?

DAY 32

HOW DO YOU ACT WHEN YOU LOSE AT SOMETHING?

DAY 33

WHAT IS THE COOLEST INVENTION YOU'VE EVER SEEN?

DAY 34

IS THERE A TIME YOU FELT LEFT OUT?

DAY 35

WHAT IS A SILLY THING YOU USED TO DO WHEN YOU WERE YOUNGER?

DAY 36

WHAT MAKES YOU FEEL NERVOUS AND WHAT DO YOU DO?

DAY 37

WHICH FRUIT OR VEGETABLE DO YOU THINK IS THE HEALTHIEST? WHY IS THAT?

DAY 38

DO YOU HAVE A HIDING PLACE?

DAY 39

USE 5 WORDS TO DESCRIBE YOURSELF.

DAY 40

WOULD YOU RATHER GET GOOD GRADES OR BE GOOD AT SPORTS?

DAY 41

WHAT IS THE ONE WISH IN THE ENTIRE WORLD YOU WOULD WISH FOR?

DAY 42

DO YOU WANT TO DRIVE A RACECAR OR FLY AN AIRPLANE?

DAY 43

HOW WOULD YOUR TEACHER DESCRIBE YOU?

DAY 44

WHEN IS A TIME SOMEONE ASKED YOU FOR FORGIVENESS?

DAY 45

DO YOU CONSIDER YOURSELF AN EXPRT AT SOMETHING? WHAT IS IT?

DAY 46

WHY DO PEOPLE LAUGH WHEN WE ARE HAPPY OR THINK SOMETHING IS FUNNY?

DAY 47

IF YOU HAD A TIME MACHINE, WOULD YOU RATHER SELL IT WITHOUT GETTING TO USE IT, OR USE IT AND NEVER GET TO SELL IT?

DAY 48

DO YOU THINK THUNDERSTORMS ARE COOL OR SCARY? OR BOTH?

DAY 49

WHO IS YOUR FAVORITE ACTOR?

DAY 50

WHAT'S YOUR FAVORITE FRUIT?

DAY 51

DO YOU LIKE DOGS OR CATS BETTER?

DAY 52

WHAT IS SOMETHING THAT'S A MYSTERY TO YOU, THAT YOU'D LIKE TO SOLVE?

DAY 53

WHAT IS THE BEST PRESENT YOU EVER GOT?

DAY 54

IF YOU COULD CHANGE YOUR SCHOOL MASCOT, WHAT WOULD YOU CHOOSE?

DAY 55

WHAT IS THE LAST GOOD DEED YOU DID?

DAY 56

WOULD YOU RATHER OWN A BOAT OR OWN AN ISLAND?

DAY 57

HOW DO YOU GET READY FOR SCHOOL IN THE MORNING?

DAY 58

DESCRIBE YOUR BEST FRIEND IN 5 WORDS.

DAY 59

WHAT'S A MOMENT IN TIME YOU WISH YOU COULD FREEZE FOREVER?

DAY 60

WHAT IS SOMETHING YOU HAD TO TRY OVER AND OVER UNTIL YOU GOT IT?

DAY 61

IS YOUR ROOM ORGANIZED OR CLUTTERED?

DAY 62

IS THERE ANYTHING YOU WISH YOU DID DIFFERENTLY IN THE PAST?

DAY 63

HAVE YOU EVER HAD TO CONVINCE SOMEONE TO DO SOMETHING?

DAY 64

WHAT DO YOU THINK IT WOULD BE LIKE IF DINOSAURS STILL EXISTED TODAY?

DAY 65

HAVE YOU WATCHED THE OLYMPICS BEFORE? WHAT WAS YOUR FAVORITE SPORT?

DAY 66

WHAT WOULD YOU ADD TO THE SCHOOL LUNCH MENU IF YOU COULD?

DAY 67

WHO IS THE BEST SUPERHERO?

DAY 68

WHAT IS YOUR FAVORITE ANIMAL?

DAY 69

WHAT IS THE MOST ANNOYING SOUND TO YOU?

DAY 70

IF YOU COULD ONLY LISTEN TO ONE TYPE OF MUSIC FOR THE REST OF YOUR LIFE, WHAT KIND WOULD IT BE?

DAY 71

WHAT IS NOT IMPORTANT TO YOU?

DAY 72

WHAT IS SOMETHING YOU COMPLAIN ABOUT OFTEN?

DAY 73

WHAT IS THE MOST INTERESTING FACT YOU KNOW?

DAY 74

WHAT IS YOUR BIGGEST FEAR?

DAY 75

WHAT DO YOU THINK IT WAS LIKE BEFORE CELL PHONES EXISTED?

DAY 76

HAVE YOU EVER GOTTEN LOST?
HOW DID IT FEEL?

DAY 77

WHAT IS SOMETHING YOU THINK TASTES GOOD THAT OTHER PEOPLE DON'T?

DAY 78

DO YOU LIKE ACTION MOVIES OR COMEDY MOVIES THE BEST?
WHY?

DAY 79

IF YOU COULD OPEN ANY KIND OF RESTAURANT, WHAT TYPE OF FOOD WOULD YOU SERVE?

DAY 80

DO YOU LIKE TAG OR HIDE-AND-GO-SEEK BETTER

DAY 81

WHAT DO YOU THINK A VOLCANO ERUPTION WOULD LOOK LIKE?

DAY 82

WHEN IS A TIME YOU WERE BRAVER THAN YOU THOUGHT YOU COULD BE?

DAY 83

IF YOU WERE A TEACHER, WHAT WOULD YOU WANT TO TEACH?

DAY 84

WHAT MOTIVATES YOU TO DO THINGS YOU ENJOY?

DAY 85

IF YOU WERE A DINOSAUR, WHICH ONE WOULD IT BE?

DAY 86

WHAT IS YOUR HAPPIEST DREAM?

DAY 87

WHAT DO YOU THINK IT WAS LIKE TO BE A CAVEMAN?

DAY 88

WHAT IS YOUR FAVORITE BOOK?

DAY 89

WOULD YOU RATHER BE COMPLETELY BALD OR COMPLETELY COVERED IN FUR?

DAY 90

DO YOU SLEEP ON YOUR BACK, STOMACH, OR SIDE?

DAY 91

WHAT IS THE MOST EXCITING THING
YOU HAVE EVER DONE?
DESCRIBE IT.

DAY 92

WHAT IS A FUN FACT ABOUT YOU MOST PEOPLE
DON'T KNOW?

DAY 93

WOULD YOU RATHER BE ABLE TO
FLY, OR SEE INTO THE FUTURE?

DAY 94

IF YOU COULD LIVE ON ANOTHER PLANET, BUT COULD NEVER COME BACK TO EARTH, WOULD YOU GO?

DAY 95

IF YOU COULD LIVE IN A MOVIE, WHICH ONE WOULD IT BE?

DAY 96

WHAT IS YOUR LEAST FAVORITE TIME OF DAY?

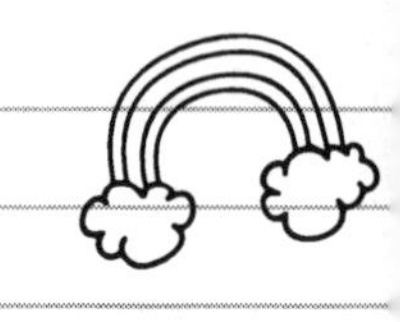

DAY 97

WHAT'S THE BEST THING THAT HAPPENED TO YOU THIS WEEK?

DAY 98

IS IT MORE IMPORTANT TO BE RICH OR TO BE KIN

DAY 99

WHAT MAKES YOU UNIQUE?

DAY 100

WHAT CLOTHES ARE YOU WEARING RIGHT NOW AND WHY?

DAY 101

DO YOU LIKE PLAYING MUSIC OR LISTENING TO MUSIC BETTER?

DAY 102

A HUGE BOX IS DELIVERED FOR YOU. WHAT DO YOU THINK IS INSIDE?

DAY 103

DO YOU THINK YOU WOULD MAKE A GOOD DETECTIVE AT SOLVING CRIMES?

DAY 104

DO YOU LIKE SPICY OR SWEET BETTER?

DAY 105

DO YOU HAVE A FAVORITE RECIPE?

DAY 106

HAVE YOU EVER CHEATED?

DAY 107

WHAT IS YOUR FAVORITE SUMMERTIME ACTIVITY?

DAY 108

IS THERE A FEAR YOU OVERCAME?

DAY 109

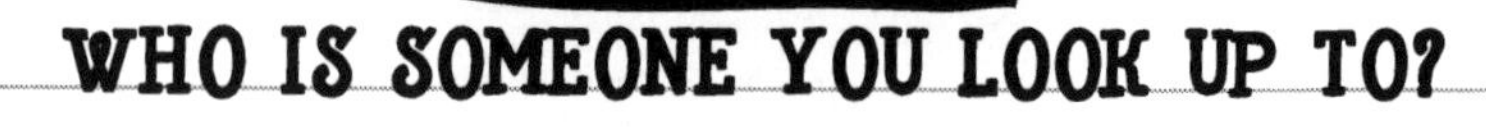

WHO IS SOMEONE YOU LOOK UP TO?

DAY 110

HAVE YOU EVER RIDDEN ON A TRAIN? WHAT WAS IT LIKE?

DAY 111

HOW DO YOU DEAL WITH UNKIND PEOPLE OR BULLIES?

DAY 112

WHAT IS YOUR LEAST FAVORITE SMELL?

DAY 113

WOULD YOU RATHER BE THE FASTEST OR THE STRONGEST PERSON ON EARTH?

DAY 114

HAVE YOU EVER ASKED SOMEONE FOR FORGIVENESS?

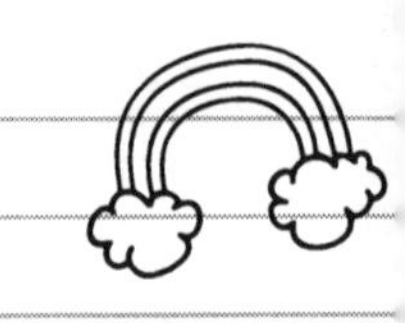

DAY 115

HOW LONG DO YOU THINK IT WOULD TAKE TO FLY TO THE END OF THE GALAXY?

DAY 116

WHAT IS IT LIKE TO FLY A KITE?

DAY 117

IF TREES COULD TALK, WHAT DO YOU THINK THEY WOULD SAY TO YOU?

DAY 118

WHY DO YOU LIKE YOUR BEST FRIEND?

DAY 119

IF YOU HAD TO ESCAPE PRISON, HOW WOULD YOU DO IT?

DAY 120

WHAT IS A TOY YOU LOVED WHEN YOU WERE YOUNGER, BUT FORGOT ABOUT?

DAY 121

IF YOU COULD BE ANY ANIMAL FOR A DAY, WHAT WOULD IT BE?

DAY 122

IF YOU HAD A REMOTE CONTROL THAT COULD TURN THE VOLUME UP OR DOWN ON ONE THING WHAT WOULD THAT THING BE?

DAY 123

WHAT MAKES YOU LAUGH?

DAY 124

WHAT MAKES YOU FEEL UPSET?

DAY 125

HOW LONG DO YOU THINK IT WOULD TAKE TO WALK ACROSS THE WHOLE COUNTRY?

DAY 126

WHAT WOULD YOUR PIRATE NAME BE?

DAY 127

HAVE YOU EVER BEEN JEALOUS OF SOMEONE?

DAY 128

DO YOU THINK IT WOULD BE FUN TO LIVE ON A SAILBOAT FOR A YEAR?

DAY 129

WOULD YOU RATHER LIVE ON THE BEACH OR ON A MOUNTAIN?

DAY 130

WHO IS SOMEONE YOU MISS?

DAY 131

WHEN IS A TIME SOMEONE WAS SAD AND YOU MADE THEM FEEL BETTER?

DAY 132

WHAT IS A HEALTHY THING YOU DO REGULARLY?

DAY 133

WHAT WOULD YOU DO IF AN ANIMAL COULD TALK TO YOU?

DAY 134

WOULD YOU RATHER NEVER EAT CAKE AGAIN, OR HAVE TO EAT ONLY CAKE FOR THE REST OF YOUR LIFE?

DAY 135

IF YOU COULD CLONE YOURSELF, WOULD YOU?

DAY 136

WHAT IS THE NICEST THING YOU EVER DID FOR SOMEONE ELSE?

DAY 137

WHAT DO YOU WISH YOU COULD CHANGE ABOUT THE WORLD?

DAY 138

WHAT IS THE NICEST THING SOMEONE ELSE DID FOR YOU?

DAY 139

WOULD YOU RATHER BE THE HERO OR THE VILLAIN?

DAY 140

DO YOU THINK PEOPLE WILL LIVE ON MARS DURING YOUR LIFETIME?

DAY 141

IF YOU COULD SEE THROUGH OBJECTS, WOULD YOU TELL ANYONE?

DAY 142

WHY DO YOU THINK PEOPLE SNEEZE?

DAY 143

HAVE YOU EVER USED A PAYPHONE?

DAY 144

YOU COULD ONLY CHOOSE HOT OR COLD WATER FOR BOTH DRINKING AND SHOWERING, WHICH WOULD YOU CHOOSE?

DAY 145

WHAT IS YOUR FAVORITE TIME OF DAY?

DAY 146

HOW DO YOU SAY "NO" TO A FRIEND WHO WANTS YOU TO DO SOMETHING YOU SHOULDN'T?

DAY 147

WHO IS THE FUNNIEST PERSON YOU KNOW?

DAY 148

WHAT'S A PROJECT OR THING YOU HAVEN'T COMPLETED YET?

DAY 149

DO YOU HAVE A SCRAPBOOK? WHAT WOULD YOU KEEP IN IT?

DAY 150

WHAT IS YOUR FAVORITE SOUND?

DAY 151

DO YOU EVER BREAK THE RULES?

DAY 152

WRITE ABOUT SOMEONE YOU ADMIRE.

DAY 153

DO YOU LIKE THE MORNING OR EVENING BETTER?

DAY 154

WHAT IS THE BEST THING ABOUT YOU?

DAY 155

WHY DO YOU THINK PEOPLE THINK THE DARK IS SCARY?

DAY 156

DO YOU LIKE GIVING GIFTS OR RECEIVING THEM BETTER?

DAY 157

WHAT IS THE MOST DIFFICULT CHOICE
YOU EVER HAD TO MAKE?

DAY 158

DO YOU LIKE READING BOOKS OR PLAYING OUTS
MORE?

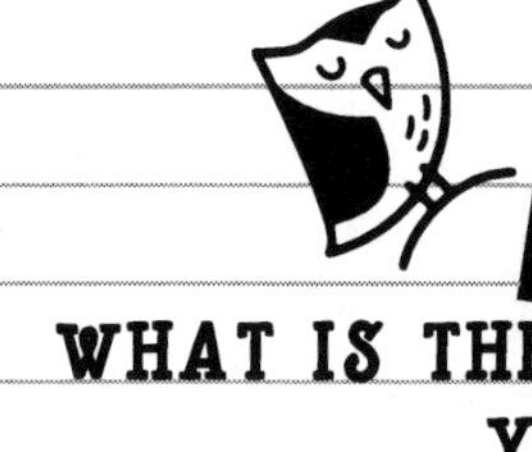

DAY 159

WHAT IS THE MOST SURPRISING THING
YOU EVER SAW?

DAY 160

HOW DO YOU HANDLE A SITUATION WHEN SOMEONE DISAGREES WITH YOU?

DAY 161

WHAT DO YOU THINK IT WOULD BE LIKE IF YOU LIVED 500 YEARS?

DAY 162

DO YOU LIKE SCIENCE OR MATH BETTER? WHY?

DAY 163

WOULD YOU RATHER BE TOO HOT OR TOO COLD?

DAY 164

WHAT IS YOUR PERSONALITY LIKE?

DAY 165

WHO IS SOMEONE THAT YOU THINK LOOKS UP TO YOU?

DAY 166

WHAT INSPIRES YOU TO DO WHAT YOU LIKE?

DAY 167

WHAT IS YOUR FAVORITE SMELL?

DAY 168

IF YOU COULD WRITE ONE NEW LAW, WHAT WOULD IT BE?

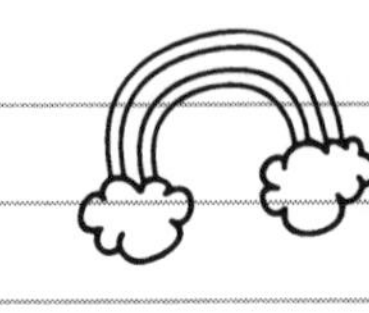

DAY 169

WHAT IS YOUR FAVORITE VEGETABLE?

DAY 170

WHAT DOES IT FEEL LIKE TO APOLOGIZE WHEN YOU ARE WRONG?

DAY 171

WHAT IS SOMETHING YOU WANT TO GET BETTER AT?

DAY 172

HOW DO YOU GET BETTER AT SUBJECTS IN SCHOOL YOU STRUGGLE WITH?

DAY 173

DO YOU LIKE LOUD PARTIES OR CONCERTS, OR PREFER IT TO BE QUIET AND UNCROWDED?

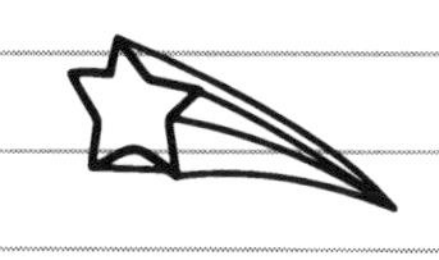

DAY 174

WHAT DO YOU THINK WILL BE THE MOST IFFERENT THING ABOUT THE FUTURE THAN NOW?

DAY 175

WHO WAS YOUR FAVORITE TEACHER SO FAR?

DAY 176

WHY DO YOU THINK PEOPLE GET OLDER?

DAY 177

DESCRIBE A TIME SOMEONE NEEDED HELP AND YOU HELPED THEM.

DAY 178

DO YOU LIKE APPLES OR ORANGES BETTER?

DAY 179

WHAT IS THE ONE THING YOU HOPE TO DO SOMEDAY?

DAY 180

WHAT MAGICAL POWER WOULD YOU CHOOSE IF YOU COULD?

DAY 181

DO YOU LIKE CAMPING?
WHY OR WHY NOT?

DAY 182

WHAT TECHNOLOGY DO YOU THINK WILL BE
INVENTED SOON?

DAY 183

IF YOU OWNED A STORE THAT COULD
ONLY SELL RED COLORED ITEMS, LIST 5
THINGS YOU'D INCLUDE.

DAY 184

HOW LONG CAN YOU HOLD YOUR BREATH?

DAY 185

DO YOU THINK ZOMBIES OR VAMPIRES WOULD BE SCARIER IF THEY WERE REAL?

DAY 186

IF YOU COULD CREATE AN ANIMAL, WHAT WOULD IT BE?

DAY 187

WHY DO YOU THINK PEOPLE LIKE DOING SCARY THINGS LIKE PARACHUTING OUT OF AN AIRPLANE?

DAY 188

DO YOU LIKE THE ZOO OR A MUSEUM BETTER?

DAY 189

DO YOU GET EASILY DISTRACTED?

DAY 190

WHAT PROMISE HAVE YOU MADE TO SOMEONE?

DAY 191

WHAT IS YOUR LEAST FAVORITE CHORE?

DAY 192

WHO IS YOUR FAVORITE PERSON FROM HISTORY YOU'VE LEARNED ABOUT IN SCHOOL?

DAY 193

DO YOU LIKE STAYING UP LATE, OR WAKING UP EARLY?

DAY 194

IF ALIENS EXIST, WOULD YOU WANT TO MEET THEM?

DAY 195

WHAT'S SOMETHING THAT'S EASY FOR YOU TO DO?

DAY 196

HOW DO YOU FEEL WHEN SOMEONE COMPLIMENTS YOU?

DAY 197

IF YOU TOOK ALL THE CONCRETE IN THE WORLD AND PUT IT TOGETHER, HOW BIG DO YOU THINK IT WOULD BE?

DAY 198

HAVE YOU EVER GOTTEN CAUGHT DOING SOMETHING YOU WEREN'T SUPPOSED TO?

DAY 199

WHAT IS YOUR FAVORITE THING ON A PLAYGROUND?

DAY 200

WHAT DO YOU THINK IT MEANS TO BE BRAVE? CAN YOU GIVE AN EXAMPLE OR DEFINITION?

DAY 201

WHAT IS YOUR FAVORITE SUBJECT IN SCHOOL?

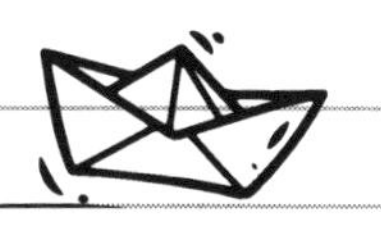

DAY 202

WHY DO YOU THINK PEOPLE LIKE YOU?

DAY 203

WHAT IS SOMETHING COOL YOU FOUND?

DAY 204

DO YOU LIKE SCARY STORIES OR FUNNY STORIES?

DAY 205

WOULD YOU RATHER LOSE YOUR SENSE OF SMELL, OR SENSE OF TASTE?

DAY 206

WHAT DO YOU THINK DOGS DREAM ABOUT?

DAY 207

IF YOU HAD TO CHOOSE ONLY ONE DESSERT FOR THE REST OF YOUR LIFE, WHAT IT WOULD BE?

DAY 208

DO YOU HAVE A LOUD VOICE OR QUIET VOICE?

DAY 209

IF YOU WORKED AT THE ZOO, WHICH ANIMAL WOULD YOU WANT TO GET TO TAKE CARE OF?

DAY 210

DO YOU LIKE RUNNING OR SWIMMING BETTER?

DAY 211

IF YOU COULD ADD ANYTHING TO YOUR HOUSE, WHAT WOULD IT BE?

DAY 212

WHAT'S SOMETHING GOOD THAT HAPPENED TO YOU THAT YOU DIDN'T THINK WAS GOOD AT THE TIME?

DAY 213

WHAT IS A RISK YOU TOOK BEFORE?

DAY 214

IF YOU COULD TRADE PLACES WITH ANYONE, WHO WOULD IT BE?

DAY 215

WHAT 3 THINGS MAKE YOU MOST HAPPY?

DAY 216

WHAT TOPPINGS DO YOU LIKE ON PIZZA?

DAY 217

DO YOU LIKE ROLLER COASTERS OR WATER SLIDES THE MOST?

DAY 218

HOW DO YOU GET PEOPLE TO COOPERATE WITH YOU?

DAY 219

IF YOU COULD BE PRESIDENT OF THE UNITED STATES, WHAT WOULD YOU DO?

DAY 220

DO YOU WANT TO CLIMB THE HIGHEST MOUNTAIN SOMEDAY?

DAY 221

HOW DO YOU STAY FOCUSED ON YOUR GOALS?

DAY 222

WHAT'S THE LONGEST LINE YOU'VE EVER WAITED IN?

DAY 223

DO YOU PREFER BIG CITIES OR SMALL TOWNS?

DAY 224

WHAT IS THE BEST GIVE YOU EVER GAVE SOMEO

DAY 225

WHAT IS YOUR FAVORITE THING TO SEE AT A MUSEUM?

DAY 226

WHAT IS SOMETHING YOU TRY TO DO EVERY DAY?

DAY 227

WHAT DO YOU THINK THE HARDEST PART OF BEING AN ADULT IS?

DAY 228

IF YOU COULD BE BETTER AT ONE THING, WHAT WOULD IT BE?

DAY 229

WHAT IS SOMETHING YOU HOPE NEVER HAPPENS TO YOU?

DAY 230

WHAT DO YOU DAYDREAM MOST OFTEN ABOUT?

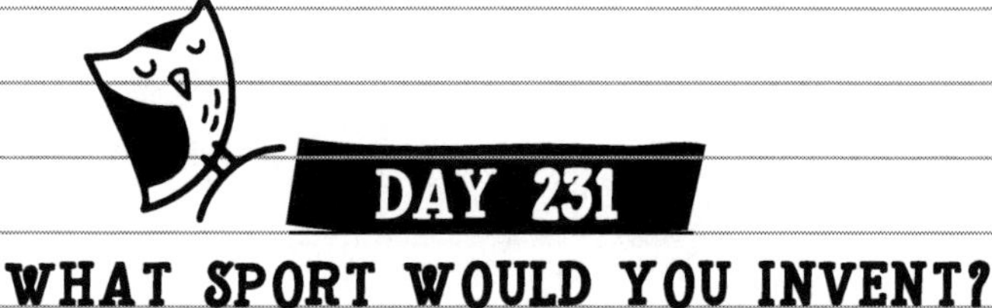

DAY 231

WHAT SPORT WOULD YOU INVENT?

DAY 232

WHAT ARE YOU MOST PROUD OF?

DAY 233

WHO IS SOMEONE YOU WISH YOU KNEW?

DAY 234

WHAT IS SOMETHING COOL YOU DISCOVERED?

DAY 235

WHAT IS YOUR FAVORITE SONG?

DAY 236

IF YOU COULD FIX ONE PROBLEM IN THE WORLD WHAT WOULD YOU DO?

DAY 237

WHAT IS SOMETHING YOU USED TO BE AFRAID OF WHEN YOU WERE YOUNGER, BUT ARE NOT AFRAID OF ANYMORE?

DAY 238

HOW DO YOU MAKE OTHER PEOPLE FEEL BETTER IF THEY ARE SAD?

DAY 239

WHAT IS A FOOD YOU'VE NEVER TRIED BUT WOULD LIKE TO?

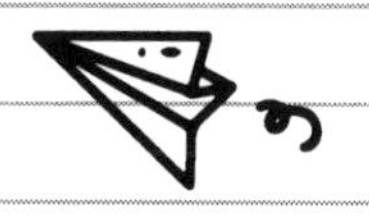

DAY 240

WOULD YOU RATHER HAVE TO EAT WORM OR YOUR LEAST FAVORITE VEGETABLE?

DAY 241

WHAT IS YOUR FAVORITE KIND OF ART TO DO?

DAY 242

WHAT'S THE WEIRDEST DREAM YOU CAN REMEMBER HAVING?

DAY 243

DO YOU LIKE EXERCISING?

DAY 244

WOULD YOU RATHER HAVE 1,000 FRIENDS OR 10 FRIENDS?

DAY 245

WHY DO PEOPLE CRY WHEN THEY ARE SAD?

DAY 246

WHAT WOULD YOU NAME A ROBOT IF YOU HAD ONE?

DAY 247

WHAT IS YOUR MOST FAVORITE FOOD?

DAY 248

IF YOU COULD ONLY CHOOSE ONE DRINK FOR TH
REST OF YOUR LIFE, WHAT WOULD YOU CHOOSE

DAY 249

WHAT IS SOMETHING YOU WOULD NEVER CHANGE ABOUT YOURSELF?

DAY 250

IF YOU WERE AN ANIMAL LIVING IN THE JUNGLE, WHICH ANIMAL WOULD YOU WANT TO BE?

DAY 251

WHAT ARE YOU LOOKING FORWARD TO MOST THIS YEAR?

DAY 252

IF YOU COULD MAKE YOUR OWN THEME PARK, WHAT KIND OF RIDES WOULD YOU CHOOSE?

DAY 253

WHAT IS YOUR FAVORITE WAY TO TRAVEL?

DAY 254

WHAT PLACE IN THE WORLD DO YOU WANT TO VISIT THE MOST?
WHY?

DAY 255

WHAT'S THE HAPPIEST MEMORY YOU HAVE?

DAY 256

IF YOU HAD $100 TO SPEND RIGHT NOW, WHAT WOULD YOU BUY?

DAY 257

WOULD YOU RATHER NEVER BE ABLE TO TELL A LIE OR NEVER BE ABLE TO TELL THE TRUTH AGAIN?

DAY 258

WHAT THINGS DO YOU DO TO KEEP YOUR BODY AND BRAIN HEALTHY?

DAY 259

WHAT TIPS WOULD YOU GIVE KIDS IN THE GRADE BELOW YOU?

DAY 260

WHAT DOES IT FEEL LIKE WHEN SOMEONE APOLOGIZES TO YOU?

DAY 261

DO YOU LIKE FICTION OR NONFICTION BOOKS BETTER?

DAY 262

WRITE ABOUT A TIME YOU OVERCAME A CHALLENGE.

DAY 263

WHAT IS SOMETHING YOU WISH YOU COULD DO MORE OFTEN?

DAY 264

HOW DO YOU DECIDE TO TRUST SOMEONE WITH A SECRET?

DAY 265

WHAT DO YOU THINK IT WILL BE LIKE TO BE AN ADULT?

DAY 266

WHAT IS THE FUNNIEST THING YOU EVER SAW

DAY 267

WHAT GOALS DO YOU WANT TO ACCOMPLISH SOMEDAY?

DAY 268

IF YOU WERE A CHARACTER IN A MOVIE, WHO WOULD IT BE?

DAY 269

WHO IS YOUR BEST FRIEND AND WHY?

DAY 270

WHAT WOULD BE YOUR LEAST FAVORITE JOB TO HAVE AS AN ADULT?

DAY 271

HOW DO YOU DEAL WITH DISAPPOINTMENT?

DAY 272

WHAT KIND OF SHOES DO YOU LIKE BEST?

DAY 273

IF YOU WERE A JOURNALIST, WHAT KIND OF STORIES WOULD YOU WANT TO WRITE ABOUT FOR THE NEWS?

DAY 274

WRITE ABOUT ONE OF YOUR NEIGHBORS.

DAY 275

WHAT WOULD YOU DO IF YOU WERE STRANDED ON AN ISLAND?

DAY 276

DO YOU WANT TO GO TO COLLEGE? WHERE?

DAY 277

WOULD YOU RATHER BE A FAMOUS ACTOR OR SPORTS STAR?

DAY 278

WHAT DO YOU DO WHEN YOU'RE BORED?

DAY 279

IF YOU HAD TO REARRANGE THE LETTERS IN YOUR NAME, WHAT WOULD YOUR NEW NAME BE?

DAY 280

MAKE UP A SILLY RHYME.

DAY 281

DO YOU LIKE TO LEAD OR FOLLOW SOMEONE ELSE?

DAY 282

HAS ANYONE EVER LIED TO YOU?

DAY 283

IF YOU WERE A ROCK STAR, WHAT WOULD YOUR BAND BE NAMED?

DAY 284

HOW DO YOU MAKE NEW FRIENDS?

DAY 285

IF YOU COULD HAVE ANY PET, WHAT KIND OF ANIMAL WOULD IT BE?

DAY 286

IF YOU HAD TO SWITCH PLACES WITH SOMEONE, WHO WOULD IT BE?

DAY 287

WHAT IS SOMETHING OTHER PEOPLE ARE AFRAID OF BUT YOU ARE NOT?

DAY 288

CAN YOU WRITE A STORY USING ONLY 12 WORDS?

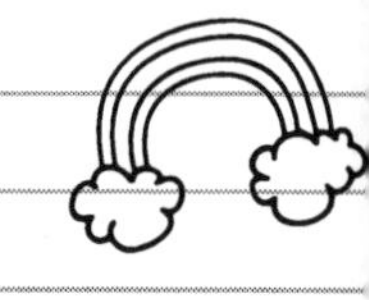

DAY 289

WHAT IS THE SCARIEST THING YOU EVER DID?

DAY 290

DO YOU HAVE ANY SECRETS?

DAY 291

WHO IS THE LAST PERSON YOU HUGGED?

DAY 292

WHAT IS A HABIT YOU WANT TO BREAK?

DAY 293

WHAT IS YOUR LEAST FAVORITE FOOD?

DAY 294

WHAT IS SOMETHING NEW YOU WANT TO TRY THIS YEAR?

DAY 295

DO YOU HAVE ANY HABITS YOU WANT TO START?

DAY 296

WHAT NEW JOBS DO YOU THINK WILL EXIST SOMEDAY THAT DON'T YET?

DAY 297

WHAT IS THE GROSSEST INSECT?

DAY 298

WHAT IS SOMETHING YOU JUST COULD NOT LIVE WITHOUT?

DAY 299

WHAT IS YOUR FAVORITE JOKE?

DAY 300

IF YOU COULD SPEAK ANY OTHER LANGUAGE IN THE WORLD, WHICH ONE WOULD YOU CHOOSE?

DAY 301

DO YOU THINK IT IS FUN TO DRIVE A CAR?

DAY 302

WHY DO YOU THINK PEOPLE HAVE TO SLEEP?

DAY 303

WHAT WOULD YOU DO IF YOU COULD TURN INVISIBLE?

DAY 304

WHAT IS YOUR FAVORITE COLOR?

DAY 305

IF YOU COULD TRAVEL TO ANYTIME IN THE PAST, WHAT WOULD YOU WANT TO SEE?

DAY 306

HOW DO YOU FEEL NOW? EXCITED OR TIRED?

DAY 307

DESCRIBE A FANTASY WORLD YOU WISH YOU COULD VISIT.

DAY 308

WHO IS YOUR FAVORITE MUSICIAN OR BAND?

DAY 309

WHY DO YOU THINK PEOPLE DREAM?

DAY 310

WHAT IS YOUR FAVORITE HOLIDAY?

DAY 311

HAVE YOU EVER TOLD A LIE?

DAY 312

DO YOU LIKE PUZZLES OR BOARD GAMES BETTER?

DAY 313

WRITE ABOUT NOT GIVING UP AND HOW YOU DO IT.

DAY 314

IF YOU COULD PAINT YOUR ENTIRE HOUSE A COLOR, WHAT WOULD IT BE?

DAY 315

WHAT ARE 3 IDEAS OF SOMETHING KIND YOU CAN DO FOR OTHERS THIS WEEK?

DAY 316

WHAT IS YOUR GREATEST STRENGTH?

DAY 317

HAVE YOU EVER SACRIFICED SOMETHING TO HELP SOMEONE ELSE?

DAY 318

WHAT IS YOUR FAVORITE PLACE TO GO?

DAY 319

WHAT DO YOU THINK IT WOULD BE LIKE
TO WALK ON THE MOON?

DAY 320

IF YOU WENT TO WORK WITH ONE OF YOUR PAREN
WHAT DO YOU THINK THE DAY WOULD BE LIKE

DAY 321

IF YOU COULD TALK TO ANIMALS OR MIND-READ
OTHER PEOPLE, WHICH WOULD YOU CHOOSE?

DAY 322

WOULD YOU RATHER BE A GREAT SINGER OR GREAT DANCER?

DAY 323

WHAT DO YOU LOVE MOST ABOUT YOUR PARENTS?

DAY 324

WOULD YOU RATHER HAVE A PIG'S NOSE OR A MONKEY'S TAIL?

DAY 325

WOULD YOU RATHER CELEBRATE CHRISTMAS OR YOUR BIRTHDAY?

DAY 326

WHAT IS THE MOST RELAXING THING YOU'VE EVER DONE?

DAY 327

WHAT HOBBY WOULD YOU LIKE TO START DOING?

DAY 328

DO YOU THINK YOU HAVE GOOD MANNERS?

DAY 329

HOW WOULD OTHER PEOPLE DESCRIBE YOU?

DAY 330

WHERE DO YOU WANT TO LIVE SOMEDAY?

DAY 331

WHAT IS YOUR DAILY ROUTINE?
WRITE OUT WHAT YOU DO EACH DAY.

DAY 332

HAVE YOU EVER LOST SOMETHING IMPORTANT TO YOU?

DAY 333

HAVE YOU EVER FELT LONELY?
WHAT MADE YOU FEEL THAT WAY?

DAY 334

WHAT ARE YOU MOST GRATEFUL FOR?

DAY 335

DO YOU LIKE BEING ALONE OR WITH A GROUP MORE?

DAY 336

HOW DO YOU ACT WHEN YOU WIN A GAME?

DAY 337

WOULD YOU WANT TO SHRINK DOWN TO THE SIZE OF AN ANT FOR ONE DAY?

DAY 338

WHAT IS THE WEATHER OUTSIDE RIGHT NOW? DOES IT INSPIRE YOU TO DO ANYTHING?

DAY 339

WHAT IS A STORY OR MOVIE YOU THINK SHOULD HAVE HAD A DIFFERENT ENDING?

DAY 340

WHAT IS THE FIRST MEMORY YOU CAN THINK OF?

DAY 341

DO YOU GET EMBARRASSED EASILY?

DAY 342

IF YOU WROTE A BOOK, WHAT WOULD IT BE ABOUT?

DAY 343

HOW DO YOU RELAX WHEN YOU FEEL STRESSED?

DAY 344

WOULD YOU RATHER SWIM AT THE POOL OR IN THE OCEAN?

DAY 345

WHAT IS YOUR FAVORITE HOLIDAY TRADITION?

DAY 346

WOULD YOU RATHER SIT OR STAND AT YOUR DESK DURING THE DAY?

DAY 347

WHAT IS THE MOST VALUABLE THING TO YOU?

DAY 348

IF ALL THE GROCERY STORES DISAPPEARED, HOW WOULD YOU GET FOOD?

DAY 349

WOULD YOU RATHER HAVE TO LIVE 100 YEARS IN THE PAST, OR 100 YEARS IN THE FUTURE?

DAY 350

WHEN IS THE LAST TIME YOU GOT A PIECE O MAIL?

DAY 351

IF YOU COULD TRAVEL TO THE MOON, WOULD YOU?

DAY 352

WHAT TECHNOLOGY DO YOU WISH EXISTED?

DAY 353

WHEN IS A TIME YOU WERE SO CLOSE TO DOING SOMETHING, BUT DIDN'T FINISH?

DAY 354

WHAT DO YOU WORRY ABOUT?

DAY 355

DO YOU LIKE WINTER OR SUMMER THE BEST?

DAY 356

DO YOU NEED AN ALARM CLOCK, OR JUST WAKE UP ON YOUR OWN?

DAY 357

DO YOU LIKE MUSIC OR SPORTS BEST? WHY?

DAY 358

WHO DO YOU LOVE MOST IN THE WORLD?

DAY 359

WHAT IS THE COOLEST THING IN YOUR GARAGE?

DAY 360

WHAT IS YOUR LUCKY NUMBER AND WHY?

DAY 361

WHAT WOULD YOU DO ON THE BEST DAY EVER?

DAY 362

WHAT KIND OF MUSIC DO YOU NOT LIKE?

DAY 363

DO YOU WANT A CAREER SOMEDAY WHERE YOU GET TO WORK OUTSIDE?

DAY 364

WHO IS YOUR FAVORITE TEACHER?

DAY 365

WHEN IS A TIME YOU SAID "NO", BUT WISH YOU SAID "YES"?

Made in the USA
Columbia, SC
16 May 2020